Our Sun

by Margie Burton, Cathy French, and Tammy Jones

Table of Contents

What Is the Sun?

The sun is a star.
It is very hot.
It is very bright.

A star is a ball of hot gas. It gives off heat and light.

The sun is very hot. We like to lie outside in the sun. The sun keeps us warm when we are outside.

The sun is a star that is near the earth. It is the only star that is so near to us that we can feel its heat.

The sun is very bright. We like to put on sunglasses when we go outside.
The light from the sun is very, very bright.

The light can hurt your eyes if you look right at it. Even when you have sunglasses on, you should not look at the sun.

Why Do We Need the Sun?

We cannot live without the sun.
We would be very cold without the sun.

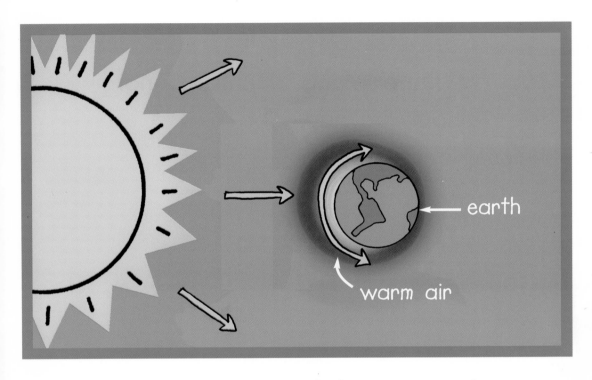

The sun warms the earth and the air around the earth. The warm air around the earth helps us stay warm.

Look at these plants. Plants cannot live without the sun. The sun helps plants grow.

We cannot live without plants. Plants give
us food to eat. Plants give us oxygen to breathe.

The sun helps make our weather, too.

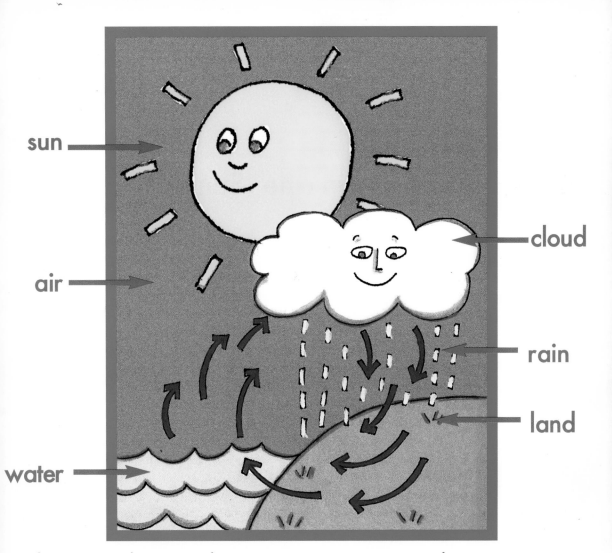

sun

air

water

cloud

rain

land

The sun's heat makes water go up into the air.
The water makes clouds. The clouds make rain.
The rain falls back to the earth.

Why Is It Hot in the Summer?

It is hot in the summer. We get a lot of the sun's light in the summer.

sun

earth

The earth travels around the sun in space.
The part of the earth that is tilted toward the sun
is having summer.

Why Do We Have Day and Night?

The earth goes around and around.

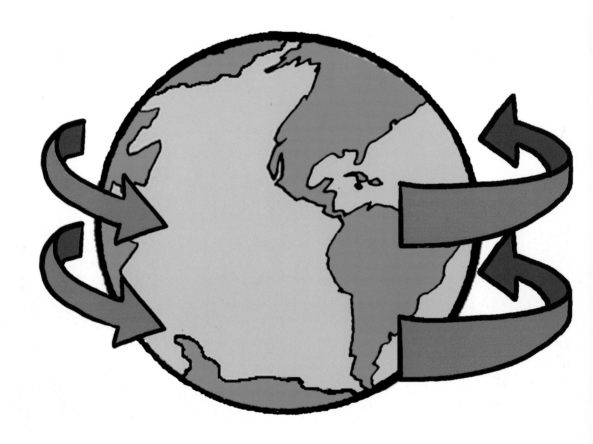

It takes the earth almost 24 hours
to turn around once.

We have day when we face the sun.

We have night when we face away from the sun.

We cannot live without the sun.